Original title:
Heart's Compass

Copyright © 2024 Swan Charm
All rights reserved.

Author: Olivia Orav
ISBN HARDBACK: 978-9916-89-880-2
ISBN PAPERBACK: 978-9916-89-881-9
ISBN EBOOK: 978-9916-89-882-6

Light Beyond the Shadows

In darkness veiled, a flame will rise,
Guiding souls toward the skies.
With whispers soft, the truth unfolds,
A light within, our hearts it holds.

Through trials faced, we seek the way,
In creased brows and in words we pray.
The shadows bend beneath His grace,
In every tear, His warm embrace.

The Celestial Call of the Heart

Beyond the stars, a voice divine,
Calls to the weary, the lost, the blind.
In every heartbeat, His love flows,
In silence deep, His essence grows.

A tapestry woven with threads of light,
Guiding the seekers through endless night.
With open hearts, we heed the plea,
To dance with grace in purity.

Embracing the Divine Flow

In rivers of faith, we come alive,
Embracing the rush, we learn to thrive.
With every breath, a sacred quest,
To find the peace, to know the blessed.

The universe sings a gentle song,
In harmony, we all belong.
Through trials faced, we find our way,
Embracing the dawn of each new day.

Soulful Wandering in Sacred Realms

In sacred realms where spirits dwell,
We wander free, we bow, we swell.
With every prayer, a path is laid,
In reverie, our doubts allayed.

The stars above, a guide so bright,
Illuminating fate's delight.
With open arms, we greet the morn,
Soulful journeys, forever reborn.

Guiding Stars in Faith's Embrace

In darkness, love's light shines bright,
Guiding souls through the night.
Each prayer a star in the sky,
Whispers of hope lifting high.

With hands clasped in humble plea,
Hearts unite, forever free.
In faith's embrace, we find our way,
A sacred path, come what may.

The Footprints of Grace

Upon the sand, a story unfolds,
Footprints of grace, in warmth, they hold.
In trials faced, we find our might,
Walking with love, through day and night.

Each step a lesson, softly spun,
In shadows where the light begun.
With every stride, the spirit grows,
Through every challenge, wisdom flows.

Vestiges of Joy in Reverence

In quiet moments, joy appears,
Filling hearts, dispelling fears.
Rays of laughter, like soft chimes,
Echoing through the sands of time.

In reverence, we find our song,
A melody where all belong.
With open arms, the spirit calls,
In joy's embrace, together falls.

The Prayerful Trail of Existence

Each breath a prayer, a sacred rite,
Guiding us toward the light.
In every moment, grace bestowed,
A gentle path where love is sowed.

With every heartbeat, souls align,
Intertwined in love divine.
The trail of life, a holy quest,
In prayerful steps, we find our rest.

Destiny's Guiding Light

In shadows deep, a beacon shines,
A path laid forth by hands divine.
With faith as wings, our spirits soar,
Embracing love forevermore.

Each step we take, the stars align,
In every heart, a truth will bind.
The journey's road, though steep and long,
Will lead us to our sacred song.

In trials faced, we find our grace,
With every tear, a warm embrace.
The light we seek, though faint at first,
Will quench our souls, fulfill our thirst.

Like rivers flow, our hopes unite,
In endless faith, we find our sight.
In prayerful whispers, dreams ignite,
Our spirits dance in destiny's light.

The Inner Sanctum's Path

In silence dwells the heart's retreat,
Where spirit's song and stillness meet.
The sacred space, it calls us near,
A whispered truth to calm our fear.

Each breath a prayer, we gather close,
In love's embrace, we find our host.
The inner light will guide our ways,
Through darkest nights and brightest days.

With every step, the journey grows,
The gift of faith in each of those.
Amidst the chaos, peace will rise,
And lead us home to tranquil skies.

In sacred trust, our souls align,
A path adorned with love divine.
Through trials faced, we shall emerge,
As seekers bound, together surge.

Echoes of Sacred Longing

In whispered prayers, the echoes flow,
Of sacred longings, heartbeats grow.
A yearning soul reaching above,
In search of peace, and searching love.

Each moment holds a promise bright,
In faith's embrace, we find our light.
The echoes call, we gather round,
In unity, our hopes are found.

As mountains stand, so firm and true,
We rise in love, our spirits renew.
The sacred song within us sings,
A tapestry of wondrous things.

Through every joy and every pain,
The echoes whisper hope again.
In silent nights and sunlit dawns,
Our sacred longings carry on.

Whispered Prayers of the Soul

In quiet corners, spirits blend,
With whispered prayers that never end.
Each heartbeat sings a sacred plea,
For love and light to set us free.

In shadows cast, the soul's refrain,
A chorus bound by joy and pain.
Through trials faced, we learn to trust,
In whispered prayers, our hearts adjust.

The stars above, our dreams they guide,
In faith, we walk, and never hide.
Each prayer a step upon the ground,
In love's embrace, we all are found.

With open hearts, we rise each day,
In whispered love, we find the way.
For every soul deserves the light,
A journey shared, forever bright.

A Journey Towards the Divine

In the stillness of the night,
I seek the light above,
A path that leads to grace,
A heart filled with love.

Each step I take behold,
The stars begin to shine,
Guiding weary souls,
Toward the divine.

With every whispered prayer,
I feel the spirits near,
Their echoes softly call,
A message pure and clear.

Through valleys deep and wide,
I tread with humble might,
For faith will be my guide,
In darkness, I find light.

As dawn breaks through the dark,
New hope begins to rise,
The journey to the heart,
Revealed in silent skies.

The Sacred Echoes of Being

In every breath I take,
There lies a sacred song,
A melody of love,
That carries me along.

The whispers of the wind,
Tell tales of ancient peace,
In nature's grand embrace,
My worries find release.

I feel the pulse of life,
In rivers flowing free,
Each wave a testament,
To divinity in me.

Within the quiet heart,
Sacred echoes arise,
Awakening the soul,
To see through faith-filled eyes.

Connected to the whole,
In oneness, we abide,
The sacred truth within,
A love we cannot hide.

Navigating by Faith's Flame

Through storms and trials fierce,
I hold onto the light,
A flicker in the dark,
That guides me through the night.

With faith as my compass,
I journey ever near,
The flame ignites my heart,
And calms my every fear.

Each challenge that I face,
Is met with trust anew,
For in the heart of chaos,
A path is shining through.

The waters may be rough,
But hope will see me through,
With every step I take,
I believe and renew.

And when I reach the shore,
Of peace beyond my dreams,
I'll know my soul was led,
By faith's unyielding beams.

The Radiant Horizon of Trust

In the distance gleams a light,
A horizon painted gold,
With trust I take my flight,
Through stories yet untold.

Each dawn a promise speaks,
Of blessings yet to be,
The radiant horizon,
Awaits in faith with me.

Through valleys of despair,
And mountains soaring high,
I'll walk with steady heart,
Beneath the boundless sky.

With every breath I take,
I find my spirit soar,
Trusting in the journey,
And what lies in store.

As shadows start to fade,
I lift my eyes in praise,
For on the path of trust,
Are miracles ablaze.

Celestial Directions

In the silence of the night, we call,
Stars shine bright, guiding all.
In shadows deep, our faith ignites,
Celestial paths reveal our sights.

With every breath, we seek the light,
Whispers of angels in pure flight.
Through trials faced, and tears we shed,
Each step taken, where spirits led.

Across the skies, the heavens beam,
In prayerful hearts, we dare to dream.
Divine embrace in every tear,
Celestial directions, ever near.

Through storms we wander, hands held tight,
In darkest hours, we find our might.
With grace abounding, we rise anew,
Guided by love, we journey true.

In the dance of life, we find our way,
Celestial whispers, come what may.
Our souls entwined, forever blessed,
In heavenly realms, we find our rest.

The Pilgrim's Reverie

Upon the path where shadows fade,
A pilgrim walks, unafraid.
With every step, a prayer takes flight,
In humble quest for sacred light.

A heart that seeks, a soul set free,
In the vast embrace of eternity.
Through valleys low and mountains high,
The pilgrim's dream shall never die.

With every heartbeat, whispers flow,
In timeless echoes, we come to know.
The journey's grace, through sun and rain,
Each moment cherished, joy and pain.

In reverie, the spirit soars,
Beyond the realms, to heaven's doors.
With faith our guide, we wander wide,
A sacred quest, a joyous ride.

Through trials faced, our spirits gleam,
The pilgrim's path is but a dream.
In every step, the world anew,
A canvas painted with love's hue.

Unseen Threads of Hope

In the quiet breath of dawn's embrace,
Unseen threads weave a sacred space.
With every heartbeat, grace appears,
Binding our spirits, calming fears.

Through trials faced, we find our way,
In darkness found, the light will play.
Threads of hope, in silence sewn,
A tapestry of love, our own.

In gentle hearts, compassion stirs,
Connection felt in whispered purrs.
Each moment shared, a cherished gift,
Unseen threads of hope, hearts uplift.

Across the miles, we rise and fall,
In unity, we hear love's call.
Though storms may rage and shadows creep,
The threads of hope we always keep.

In faith we stand, hands intertwined,
In love's embrace, our souls aligned.
Together bound, we journey forth,
Unseen threads of hope, our endless worth.

Chasing the Divine Rhythm

In every heartbeat, music plays,
Chasing the divine, through all our days.
With every note, our souls ignite,
In harmony, we find our light.

Through trials faced and shadows cast,
We dance to rhythms, unsurpassed.
In sacred chants and whispered prayers,
The beat of love is found everywhere.

In moments still, the spirit sways,
Guided by grace, in endless ways.
Through laughter shared, and tears we share,
Chasing the divine, in loving care.

As stars align, we follow through,
In cosmic dance, we are renewed.
With every step, our hearts shall sing,
In chorus sweet, to life we cling.

Through paths unknown, we trust the climb,
In every pulse, we chase divine.
In unity, our spirits rise,
Chasing the rhythm, beneath the skies.

The Pathway of Sacred Yearning

In the stillness of the night, I seek,
A gentle voice that softly speaks.
Guiding light on my weary way,
Leading my heart to a brighter day.

With every step, the spirit calls,
Through lush valleys and ancient halls.
In whispers sweet, the truth unfolds,
As love surrounds my heart of gold.

The light above, a beacon clear,
In every shadow, it draws me near.
With every prayer, I draw anew,
A sacred bond, my heart and you.

Through trials faced, my soul will rise,
In humble trust beneath the skies.
For all I seek is love divine,
In every heartbeat, your light will shine.

As dawn breaks through the darkened veil,
I walk the path where angels sail.
With open heart, my spirit yearns,
On this sacred path, my soul returns.

Whispers from the Celestial Horizon

From heights unseen, a gentle breeze,
Carries messages through swaying trees.
In the quietude, a truth resounds,
In whispered hopes, the love abounds.

Stars above in endless night,
Illuminate the sacred sight.
Every twinkle, a cosmic sigh,
Reminds my spirit of realms up high.

With faith as guide, I journey forth,
Seeking solace for my heart's worth.
Each step I take, the path unfolds,
A tapestry of grace that holds.

On the horizon, dreams align,
In sacred moments, hearts entwine.
Through trials faced in faith and light,
My spirit soars, taking flight.

Beneath the vast and endless sky,
I sense the presence drawing nigh.
In silent prayer, my heart's desire,
Burns bright and true, a holy fire.

The Eternal Journey Within

Within the depths of every soul,
A sacred journey makes us whole.
In quiet moments, truth reveals,
The love of God, our heart's ideals.

Through valleys low and mountains high,
In every tear and joyful sigh.
The voice of peace, it softly speaks,
In silent prayer, the spirit seeks.

With courage born of faith and grace,
I tread the path, I seek your face.
In trials faced, I find my light,
Guided by love through darkest night.

Each breath I take, a step in trust,
In every challenge, rise I must.
For in the stillness of the heart,
The sacred echoes never part.

The journey inward leads me home,
In every silence, I am known.
With open arms, I walk this grace,
And find my essence in this space.

Illuminated Steps of Faith

In the twilight of my darkest hour,
I seek the light, the holy power.
Each step I take, your grace surrounds,
In faith, I walk on sacred grounds.

The path ahead, with light aglow,
Illuminates the seeds I sow.
With every doubt that clouds my mind,
In quiet prayer, your peace I find.

Through storms that shake, I stand my ground,
In trust and love, my heart is bound.
For every challenge, I embrace,
Illuminated by your grace.

Upon this journey, hand in hand,
I find my strength where I stand.
In whispered hopes and dreams pursued,
With every heartbeat, love renewed.

As sunlight breaks the morning mist,
I walk assured, I cannot resist.
With faith, I rise, and do not wane,
In illuminated steps, I remain.

Echoes of the Eternal Call

In shadows deep, a whisper flows,
A gentle nudge, where spirit grows.
The heart attunes to sacred sound,
In silence blooms, grace is found.

Through veils unseen, the path aligned,
Where love and light shall intertwine.
Each step unfolds a holy grace,
In every breath, a sacred space.

For in the night, a star will guide,
The weary soul, the heart's true tide.
With faith as compass, hope the sail,
We journey forth, where dreams prevail.

From earthly forms to realms above,
We seek the truth, we seek the love.
In every echo, a promise speaks,
Of endless joy that softly seeks.

Awake, arise, the call is clear,
Embrace the light that draws us near.
In unity, we dance and sing,
To the eternal, our souls take wing.

The Divine Road Unfolds

In morning light, the path appears,
A sacred journey, free of fears.
With every step, the vision grows,
The heart ignites, a flame that glows.

Through valleys deep, and mountains high,
The spirit soars, beneath the sky.
With trust as guide, we forge ahead,
On golden trails, where angels tread.

In moments still, we hear the prayer,
A melody that fills the air.
In every sigh, the breath of life,
Transforms the struggle, calms the strife.

The way may twist, the night may fall,
Yet love will reign, and grace will call.
Through storms and sun, the soul will roam,
For in the journey, we find home.

With every dawn, the promise shines,
A sacred truth that intertwines.
In love's embrace, we rise and stand,
The divine road leads hand in hand.

Sacred Destinations Await

In distant lands where spirits dwell,
The sacred stories weave and swell.
Each step we take, a tale unfolds,
In whispered dreams, the heart beholds.

Mountains rise, the rivers flow,
Each sacred place, we come to know.
In nature's arms, our souls align,
In every leaf, a touch divine.

With open hearts, the gifts we share,
In unity, we breathe the air.
Through laughter, tears, we find our way,
In sacred moments, night and day.

So seek the paths where love will lead,
Where each embrace assures the need.
The destinations shine with grace,
In every smile, the holy face.

Our journey holds the truth inside,
In every step, the love, our guide.
The sacred waits, with arms so wide,
For every soul on destiny's ride.

The Oracles of Intuition

In quietude, the whispers rise,
A voice within, where wisdom lies.
The heart knows truth, beyond the veil,
In every thought, a sacred trail.

With gentle nudges, spirits speak,
In moments still, we learn to seek.
In dreams at night, the visions flow,
As oracles of light bestow.

Trust in the signs, they guide the way,
Through shadows dark, to brightening day.
In every breath, a chance to heed,
The truths revealed, the soul's own creed.

When doubts arise, let love prevail,
For in the heart, we won't derail.
Each instinct leads to realms sublime,
The oracles embrace through time.

Awake, dear soul, embrace the light,
In every moment, wrong or right.
The guiding force will always beckon,
Through divine whispers, we are reckoned.

Illuminated by Spirit's Flame

In the quiet hush of night,
The stars begin to gleam.
With every pulse of light,
Awakens the holy dream.

Whispers of the ancient truth,
Dance upon the breeze.
Filling hearts with holy youth,
Setting souls at ease.

From shadows, hope will rise,
Guided by the flame.
Each prayer a soft surprise,
Calling out your name.

With fervor, let us seek,
The sacred in our midst.
In silence, we grow weak,
Embracing paths unkissed.

Together we will stand,
In harmony we dwell.
Illuminated by the hand,
Of love, our hearts will swell.

The Altar of Desire

Upon the altar, dreams reside,
With candlelight aglow.
In every longing deep inside,
Awaits the spirit's flow.

Each wish a gentle sigh,
Carried on the breeze.
The heavens catch our cry,
And grant us hearts at ease.

In fervor we confess,
The yearnings of our soul.
In love, we find our rest,
And make the broken whole.

With every tear we shed,
In passion's holy fire.
Transcend the fear and dread,
Embrace the pure desire.

So gather round with grace,
The offerings of heart.
In unity, we face,
The beauty of our art.

The Holy Cartography of Love

Maps of the heart unfold wide,
With paths of pure intent.
In every soul, love's guide,
In every moment spent.

With ink of sacred trust,
We draw the lines that bind.
In love's reflection, just,
Our destinies aligned.

Through valleys low and high,
We navigate as one.
Across the open sky,
The journey has begun.

In every hidden nook,
A treasure waits to be.
With every longing look,
We find infinity.

So let love be our map,
A compass in the dark.
In unity, we tap,
The sacred, soaring arc.

Sacred Signs in the Wilderness

In whispers, nature speaks clear,
To hearts that softly listen.
Sacred signs, we hold dear,
In each tear that glistens.

The rustle of the leaves,
Carries a holy tune.
In every breath, belief weaves,
A promise from the moon.

Through deserts dry and vast,
Each grain a lesson shared.
In every moment passed,
The spirit's path is bared.

With footsteps light and free,
We journey through the night.
In every shadow, see,
The sparks of love's own light.

So walk this way with grace,
In wilderness, we find.
The sacred signs embrace,
The peace that soothes the mind.

Signs of Grace in the Everyday

In the gentle whisper of the breeze,
We find the touch of grace that frees.
Moments glisten like the morning dew,
Each a blessing, pure and true.

In the laughter shared beneath the sun,
We glimpse the love where life begun.
Simple kindness warms the mundane,
A sacred thread in joy and pain.

In the quiet sigh of evening's glow,
The heart remembers what it knows.
Each star a sign of mercy's plan,
A promise held in heaven's span.

In the eyes of stranger passing by,
We see reflections that reach the sky.
Every encounter, a holy chance,
A dance of spirits, a sacred dance.

In the stillness, hear the prayerful call,
Inviting us to rise and stand tall.
With every heartbeat, grace aligns,
In the everyday, the divine shines.

Embracing the Divine Sanctum

Within the chapel of the heart we dwell,
Where whispers of the spirit softly swell.
Each prayer a feather, light and free,
Guiding us to sacred unity.

In the shadows where the silence grows,
The essence of truth gently shows.
A sanctuary built on faith and grace,
Embracing love in every space.

Through the veil of dreams and night's embrace,
We seek the light of divine grace.
Every moment, still and sacred ground,
In the quiet, God's presence found.

In the breaking of the morning light,
Awakens hope, dispelling night.
With open arms, we find our place,
In the divine, we embrace the grace.

Through each heartbeat and every breath,
We find the life that conquers death.
A journey inward, a sacred quest,
Emboldened by grace, we are blessed.

Divine Revelations of the Soul

In the stillness of the heart's retreat,
Awakens visions pure and sweet.
Each revelation, a spark so bright,
Illuminating paths with holy light.

In the laughter shared with cherished friends,
We glimpse the love that never ends.
Every moment a divine reveal,
Truth unfolds in layers we feel.

In the dance of leaves in autumn's air,
The beauty of change, a sacred prayer.
Each color sings of life anew,
Reminding us of the love so true.

In the whispers of the night so clear,
We hear the echoes of something near.
The soul's longing for connection, whole,
In every heartbeat, divine control.

Through trials faced and burdens shared,
We find the strength of love declared.
With each step toward the unknown goal,
We embrace the divine within our soul.

Guiding Light Through Inner Wilderness

In the depths of night where shadows creep,
A guiding light within, ours to keep.
Through wilderness of doubt and despair,
Faith shines brightly, leading us there.

In the rustle of leaves, a soft sigh,
Nature whispers to hearts that cry.
Every star a beacon in the dark,
A spark of hope ignites the stark.

Through the valleys low and mountains high,
We tread the path where eagles fly.
With each step, a sacred song we sing,
Embracing the love that seasons bring.

In the moments of solitude and fear,
The inner voice of truth draws near.
Resilient spirit, forever bold,
In the wilderness, grace unfolds.

As dawn breaks clear, the shadows fade,
We walk in light, no longer afraid.
The journey teaches, the heart refines,
Guided always, by love that aligns.

The Mystic's Chart of Aspirations

In silence, dreams take flight,
A chart unfolds by candlelight.
With every breath, a prayer is sown,
In fields of visions, seeds are grown.

Beyond the veil where whispers dwell,
The heart knows truths it cannot tell.
Each star a guide, each tear a grace,
Mapping the soul's eternal chase.

Through storms of doubt, through winds of fear,
The mystic's path is ever clear.
A tapestry of hopes entwined,
In divinity, our spirits find.

With faith as light and love as key,
A journey unfolds, wild and free.
Amidst the shadows, faith will bloom,
Illuminating the heart's own room.

The soul ascends toward the dawn,
In unity, the self is drawn.
In every moment, the truth ignites,
A mystic's chart in endless flights.

Pathways Through the Divine Whisper

In quietude, the spirit breathes,
Among the leaves, a soft heart weaves.
Each step upon the sacred ground,
In every breath, a love profound.

From mountain high to valley low,
The divine whispers, soft and slow.
In echoes of the ancient song,
We find the place where we belong.

With open hearts, we seek the signs,
In moonlit nights, the cosmos shines.
Through pathways paved in grace and light,
The soul is guided through the night.

Across the rivers of despair,
The gentle breeze still lingers there.
In every trial, a truth revealed,
In faith, our wounds are gently healed.

So take the hand of spirit's call,
Embrace the journey, cherish all.
Through divine whispers, we are blessed,
In every heartbeat, we find rest.

Finding Home in Sacred Places

In every heart, a yearning sigh,
To find the home that will not die.
Amidst the chaos, refuge waits,
In sacred places, love narrates.

Among the stones and ancient trees,
The pulse of life, a gentle breeze.
In shadows cast by moonlit grace,
We feel the warmth, we find our space.

The sacred hymn, so pure and sweet,
Guides weary souls upon their feet.
Through every trial and tear we face,
We find the light in sacred grace.

In every smile, a sacred spark,
In every soul, the love can mark.
Through unity, we become whole,
Finding home within each soul.

With every heart, a gateway wide,
In sacred places, we abide.
In love's embrace, the spirit grows,
In place of peace, the heart must flow.

The Star of Surrender

In twilight hours, the journey bends,
Each sigh a gift, the cosmos sends.
The star of surrender lights the way,
Guiding the lost, come what may.

With open arms, we gently yield,
To divine love, our spirits healed.
In every moment, we release,
The burdens fade, we find our peace.

Through valleys deep and mountains high,
The star above, our sacred sky.
In shadows cast, we learn to trust,
In every heart, the hope is just.

The night may fall, the dawn will rise,
In surrender, the spirit flies.
An ever-constant, guiding light,
Illuminating the darkest night.

With faith in heart and hope in hand,
We journey forth, a sacred band.
The star of surrender beckons near,
In love's embrace, we have no fear.

The Sacred Tides of Destiny

In the stillness of the night,
Waves whisper truths divine,
Guided by celestial light,
Where the souls intertwine.

Each star a beacon bright,
Charting paths unknown,
With faith as our guiding sight,
Our hearts are not alone.

Through valleys deep we roam,
With courage as our guide,
Each step leads us home,
To the shores of the wide.

The tides may rise and fall,
Yet still, we find our way,
In the silence, hear the call,
Embrace the light of day.

Destiny unfolds like a scroll,
Written in ancient dust,
The sacred tides touch every soul,
In this journey, we trust.

The Soul's Sacred Orientation

In the garden of the heart,
Whispers of love arise,
Each moment a sacred part,
Under the endless skies.

Tread gently on this earth,
With reverence and grace,
Each soul knows its worth,
In this sacred space.

The compass points within,
Guided by the divine,
In silence, we begin,
To seek and to align.

Lost in the world's noise,
We find our still refrain,
In the echoes, hear our joys,
Love's sweet, soft refrain.

The journey of the soul,
Is a tapestry of dreams,
As we seek the whole,
Life is more than it seems.

Ascent to the Higher Calling

Each mountain we must face,
Holds lessons etched in stone,
With every step, we trace,
The path that leads us home.

In the valleys of despair,
Hope springs eternal fast,
With each breath, feel the air,
The shadows cannot last.

A voice calls from above,
In the stillness, it grows,
With faith, rise up in love,
Embrace what the heart knows.

Hearts aflame, spirits soar,
Towards horizons bright,
With each stride, we explore,
The infinite divine light.

Echoes of the ages sing,
In unity, we rise,
To the call that life shall bring,
In truth, we realize.

The Luminous Thread of Belief

In the tapestry of time,
Threads of faith interlace,
With every joy and climb,
We find our sacred place.

Belief lights the darkest night,
A spark in the soul's core,
Guiding us towards the right,
Opening every door.

Through trials we shall learn,
With patience and with grace,
In the heart, a flame will burn,
A sacred, timeless space.

The luminous thread connects,
Us to the endless sky,
In its warmth, love reflects,
As we seek, we fly high.

With open minds and hearts,
We weave what we believe,
In each moment, precious parts,
In love, we shall achieve.

The Geography of the Spirit

In valleys deep where shadows lie,
The whispered prayers ascend on high.
Mountains tall, their peaks aglow,
With sacred winds, the spirits flow.

Rivers run, a silver thread,
Binding hearts where hope is fed.
The forests hum an ancient song,
In nature's arms, we all belong.

Beneath the stars, our souls unite,
In the vast depths of the night.
Paths of peace we tread with care,
In every breath, the sacred air.

One heart beats with the earth's own grace,
In every corner, we find our place.
Navigating through faith's embrace,
The spirit's map we all can trace.

Through every twist, the soul does soar,
In journeys deep, forevermore.
With lanterns bright, we find our way,
In each new dawn, the spirit's play.

Emblems of Faith Along the Way

Each step we take, a symbol true,
A canvas bare with love imbue.
In every heart, a story glows,
With faith's embrace, the light bestows.

From the one seed, a tree shall rise,
Bearing gifts beneath the skies.
In humble acts, the spirit's might,
In every dawn, the hope ignites.

A gentle touch, a kind refrain,
In love we pour, in joy we gain.
Emblems crafted from our tears,
Transformed to joy through love's own years.

With hands outstretched, we lift the lost,
Navigating through every cost.
A tapestry of lives entwined,
In faith's embrace, the truth we find.

The crosses worn upon our chests,
Remind us of our sacred quests.
Together, we shall stand and pray,
In every heartbeat, love's display.

The Journey Through Sacred Light

In shadows cast by fleeting night,
We seek the dawn, a hopeful sight.
Holding hands with the Divine,
We journey forth, our hearts align.

A lantern glows, a gentle guide,
Leading us where dreams abide.
With every step, a prayer unfolds,
In whispers soft, the truth it holds.

Through valleys low and mountains steep,
The sacred vows, our souls do keep.
In every trial, we stand as one,
In love and faith, our work begun.

Reflections dance on waters clear,
In every drop, the voice we hear.
Embrace the light that fills the air,
A sacred promise, beyond compare.

With joyous hearts, we shout the praise,
In every moment, time displays.
The journey rich with grace and might,
As we walk on through sacred light.

The Quest of the Faithful Heart

With steadfast steps, the faithful roam,
In search of truth, they call it home.
A heart that beats with passion's fire,
In every trial, they lift it higher.

Through deserts dry and forests vast,
The shadows whisper stories past.
Unyielding spirit, brave and bold,
In every passage, love behold.

The quest divine, a journey shared,
Each soul a spark, together bared.
In kindness sown, a garden grows,
With every tear, compassion flows.

In quiet moments, they will find,
The holy light that warms the mind.
Each faithful heart, a beacon bright,
Illuminating through the night.

With arms extended, they unite,
Chasing dreams in the moonlight.
In every heartbeat, love imparts,
The journey treasured, faithful hearts.

Starbound Journeys of the Soul

In the night sky, the stars align,
Guiding the heart to realms divine.
Each twinkling light, a whisper clear,
Calls us forth, dispels the fear.

Lost in the cosmos, we seek our way,
As celestial choirs sing and sway.
Every journey, a sacred quest,
In the vast void, our souls find rest.

Through the darkness, we walk as one,
Chasing the rays of the coming dawn.
Embracing dreams, we lift our hands,
In unity, our spirit stands.

With each heartbeat, we trace the stars,
Knowing our home lies beyond Mars.
In the arms of the endless sky,
We find our truth; we learn to fly.

The cosmos speaks in silence bold,
Tales of love and life unfold.
A journey vast, yet deeply known,
In the stars, we are not alone.

The Mystic's Leading Star

Oh, glowing orb in the silent night,
You beckon souls with gentle light.
In your presence, we seek our way,
Through shadows cast where dreamers sway.

A mystical guide in the cosmic sea,
Awakening hearts, setting spirits free.
With each twinkle, secrets unfold,
Stories of faith, eternally told.

Under your watch, we wander wide,
Navigating paths where the mystics reside.
In the embrace of your soothing beam,
We find our purpose, we dare to dream.

Through trials faced and burdens borne,
You remind us we are reborn.
A beacon bright, in darkness found,
In your wisdom, our hopes abound.

Eternal star, our spirits rise,
Guided by dreams, we touch the skies.
With gratitude, we follow your call,
In the sacred night, we heed it all.

Enigma of the Inner Light

In the stillness, a light does gleam,
A beacon bright, a whispered dream.
Within the heart, a flame ignites,
Illuminating the darkest nights.

The enigma speaks in silent grace,
Reflecting truth in every face.
As we journey through layers deep,
The inner light, our souls shall keep.

Each glimmer holds a tale to weave,
Of faith and hope for those who believe.
In shadows' clutch, we find our way,
The light within will never sway.

Through trials faced and storms weathered,
In the warmth of the light, we are tethered.
It guides our paths, it calms our fears,
The essence of love, through all our years.

With each heartbeat, we feel it rise,
A sacred rhythm beneath the skies.
In the dance of life, we find our song,
The inner light, where we belong.

Illuminating the Veiled Path

In shadows deep where footsteps tread,
A light emerges to guide the thread.
Illuminating paths once veiled,
Through every fear, our hearts are hailed.

With gentle rays, the night gives way,
To whispers of hope that softly sway.
Each step we take, with faith aligned,
The light reveals what once was blind.

Through winding roads and mazes vast,
We seek the truth that holds us fast.
In the valley of doubt, we find our trust,
As love's embrace turns stone to dust.

The veiled path holds sacred grace,
A sanctuary where dreams we trace.
In every twist, in every bend,
The light of love shall never end.

With open hearts and open minds,
We walk together; our spirit binds.
Embracing love, we shine so bright,
Illuminating the world with light.

The Sacred Journey Within

In silence deep, the heart does find,
A whisper soft, a voice so kind.
With every breath, the spirit soars,
To seek the love that ever pours.

Through trials fierce, the path is steep,
Yet faith in light begins to leap.
Each step unfolds the sacred grace,
Revealing truth in a warm embrace.

When shadows fall and doubts arise,
The inner light will pierce the skies.
Holding fast to the guiding star,
We learn just who and what we are.

In every tear, a lesson sown,
In every joy, the love we've known.
Thus, on this journey, we must trust,
For in the heart, the divine must gust.

At journey's end, when peace is near,
We find the light that calms our fear.
The sacred path has always shown,
The love within has always grown.

Grace Notes of the Spirit

In morning's light, the spirit sings,
A melody of sacred things.
Each note a prayer, each chord a dream,
Together woven, a golden seam.

With every heartbeat, grace unfolds,
A tale of love in whispers told.
The rhythm guides through joy and pain,
In harmony, we break the chain.

Through trials faced, the spirit learns,
In every setback, the fire burns.
For even storms must pass away,
To bring the dawn of a brighter day.

In every deed, a touch of light,
We lift our hearts, embrace the fight.
The grace we share, a sacred gift,
Can heal the soul, our hearts uplift.

So let us dance to faith's sweet tune,
With hope arising like the moon.
In grace, we find our truest voice,
In each small step, we make our choice.

Navigation Through Faith's Labyrinth

In shadows cast by doubt's cruel hand,
We seek the light in faith's vast land.
Each twist and turn, a challenge waits,
A sacred maze that love creates.

With every prayer, the path grows clear,
The heart knows truth when love is near.
Through darkest nights, we find our way,
A guiding star that will not sway.

Though storms may rage and winds may howl,
In faith, the spirit wears a crown.
With courage forged in trials tough,
Our souls resilient, strong enough.

Each lesson learned, a step so bold,
Within the labyrinth, tales unfold.
In sharing hearts, we break the walls,
In every voice, the spirit calls.

As light emerges from the gloom,
With love's embrace, we find our room.
In unity, our faith will thrive,
In every heart, the truth alive.

The Infinite Quest for Truth

In every question, wisdom breathes,
The quest for truth in heart believes.
With open minds, we seek to learn,
To unveil mysteries, deep and stern.

Across the ages, voices rise,
In every tale, a truth defies.
With courage found in shared pursuit,
In every step, we find the root.

Through paths of light, through shadows cast,
The soul's great journey, ever vast.
In every heart, a flicker glows,
A sacred fire that ever flows.

In every rise, a fall we face,
Yet in each trial, we find our grace.
For truth, though hidden, soon breaks free,
Revealing love in you and me.

So let us seek with fervent hope,
Through winding roads, we learn to cope.
In every moment, truth will shine,
In every heart, divine design.

Journey of the Faithful Dreamer

In the stillness of the night,
A dream awakens, pure and bright.
Guided by a gentle light,
The faithful heart begins its flight.

With every step, the hope ascends,
Through valleys deep, where sorrow bends.
Yet faith in love, forever mends,
The path unseen, the soul transcends.

Whispers of grace in shadows found,
In prayerful silence, peace abound.
The spirit speaks without a sound,
In unity, our hearts are bound.

Mountains high and rivers wide,
The faithful dreamer will abide.
With courage strong and arms spread wide,
In journey's midst, we find our guide.

As dawn breaks through the darkest hour,
Each moment blooms, a sacred flower.
With every trial, faith's sweet power,
The dreamer finds divinity's shower.

Communion with the Spirit Wind

In the breath of morning, soft and clear,
The spirit calls, its voice draws near.
In every rustle, we revere,
The sacred bond, the heart sincere.

As leaves dance free in joyful flight,
We close our eyes, embrace the light.
With open hearts, through day and night,
The spirit wind ignites our sight.

In the stillness of the sacred grove,
We find the ties that ever strove.
To know the path that love behoves,
In unity, our spirits rove.

Through mountain echoes, through ocean's sigh,
In whispered prayers, we touch the sky.
With every heartbeat, we rely,
On spirit's grace, we learn to fly.

In the twilight's glow, we find our place,
Together bound in sacred space.
In communion sweet, we interlace,
The spirit wind, our hearts embrace.

The Pilgrim's Heart

Upon the road where shadows play,
The pilgrim walks both night and day.
With every stone along the way,
A story whispered, come what may.

Through valleys wide and mountains steep,
The pilgrim's vow, a promise deep.
In faith they sow, in hope they reap,
Their journey long, the mind to keep.

Each trial faced, a lesson learned,
With every step, the fire burned.
In love's embrace, the soul returned,
For in the heart, the light discerned.

Through winding paths of joy and pain,
The pilgrim's truth, like summer rain.
In every loss, we find the gain,
In heavenly peace, we're home again.

Embracing all, from dusk till dawn,
The pilgrim's heart is never drawn.
With every mile, they carry on,
In faith, they sing the sacred song.

The Sacred Inevitable

In the tapestry of time, we weave,
The threads of fate, we all believe.
In every breath, we learn to cleave,
To love and light, the heart's reprieve.

With gentle hands, the stars align,
In cosmic dance, the souls entwine.
Through trials vast, our spirits shine,
In faith's embrace, our love divine.

Through seasons' change, the wheel turns round,
In sacred circles, truths are found.
With every heartbeat, joy unbound,
The inevitable, life's sound.

With open minds, we seek to know,
The whispers soft, the inner glow.
In every moment, love will grow,
The sacred path, we chance to show.

In the unity of all that is,
We find our peace, our sacred bliss.
In every prayer, in every kiss,
The heart embraces the eternal whir.

Resonance of the Soul's Awakening

In the stillness of dawn, light breaks,
Whispers of divinity in gentle shakes.
Hearts open wide to the soft embrace,
Awakening truths, a sacred space.

Mountains stand tall, guardians of time,
Echoes of wisdom, in rhythm and rhyme.
Nature's chorus sings a timeless tune,
Guiding the seekers beneath the moon.

The spirit dances, free as a bird,
Carried on winds, through every word.
Threads of connection weave through the haze,
Illuminating paths in mysterious ways.

Tears of joy fall like rain from the skies,
Cleansing the soul, as the spirit flies.
Each moment a gift, a divine decree,
In the resonance, we find unity.

Awakening softly, in light's embrace,
The soul's true journey, a sacred race.
With every heartbeat, a calling anew,
In the silence, the echoes break through.

The Providence of Winding Roads

Through valleys low and mountains high,
The path unfurls beneath the sky.
Each twist and turn, a lesson learned,
In faith we wander, our hearts yearned.

The compass points, though unseen and vague,
Leads us to places where spirits beg.
In every struggle, in every pain,
We find the strength to rise again.

Beneath the stars, our dreams are sown,
In whispered prayers, we are not alone.
The road may change, but faith remains,
In love's embrace, our hope retains.

As rivers flow, so too do we,
With every bend, we learn to be free.
In the dance of fate, we find our chance,
To step with grace in life's sacred dance.

vidence guides through dark and light,
h moment crafted, a divine sight.
ding roads, our souls will roam,
ng our way, forever home.

Synchronicities Along the Journey

Moments collide in a dance divine,
Stars align as our hearts entwine.
Every glance, a subtle sign,
In the tapestry of fate, we find the line.

Paths cross under the watchful night,
Guided by forces, unseen in sight.
Voices call from the depths of the soul,
In synchronicities, we feel whole.

A stranger's smile, a knowing glance,
In the chaos, we find our chance.
In whispered hints, the universe speaks,
Leading us forth, in the silence it seeks.

Through trials faced, the shadows cast,
Light breaks forth, illuminating the vast.
Each thread connected, a sacred design,
In the cosmic weave, our hearts align.

Synchronicities weave through the air,
Reminders that love is always there.
With every heartbeat, we dance with fate,
In the journey of life, love will await.

Messages from the Sacred Unknown

In the silence, a voice calls clear,
Messages spoken for those who hear.
The sacred whispers in shadows abide,
Guiding the faithful, where truths reside.

Dreams unfold like petals of grace,
Inviting the soul to embrace its place.
In still moments, the unknown reveals,
The path where the heart truly feels.

Signs in the sky, a flickering light,
Desires ignited, dispelling the night.
The sacred unknown beckons us near,
In mysteries wrapped, we conquer our fear.

Through trials and tears, the chaos of heart,
In messages whispered, we feel a new start.
In every heartbeat, a sacred decree,
The universe speaks through you and through me.

With open hearts, we journey along,
Finding our strength in the cosmic song.
Messages flourish, in love we trust,
In the sacred unknown, we are forever thrust.

The Sacred Lantern's Glow

In the night, a lantern shines,
Its gentle light divine and pure.
Guiding souls through shadowed lands,
In its warmth, we find our cure.

Each flicker tells a tale of grace,
Of prayers whispered, hearts entwined.
With every glow, we seek embrace,
In faith's embrace, our spirits bind.

The path ahead may twist and turn,
Yet through the dark, the light will gleam.
In sacred light, our hearts shall yearn,
For love's embrace, our brightest dream.

Let hope ignite the lantern's flame,
A beacon through the dusk of doubt.
With every step, we call His name,
In faith, our blessings sprout.

So carry forth the sacred light,
Through trials faced, let courage flow.
With love and faith, in darkest night,
Together, we will brightly glow.

Echoes of Faith in Life's Journey

Hear the echoes of the past,
Whispers carried on the breeze.
Voices strong and shadows cast,
In faith, we find our inner peace.

Each step we take, each path we roam,
Devotion guides our weary heart.
From distant lands, we seek a home,
In every tear, a brand new start.

The mountains high and valleys low,
Speak of truths that never die.
In every heart, belief will grow,
As faith unfolds beneath the sky.

Through trials faced, we learn to stand,
With open hearts and lifted eyes.
In unity, we join our hands,
Beneath the stars, our spirits rise.

So let the echoes softly ring,
In every heart, let love abide.
Through faith, each soul shall learn to sing,
As we walk, forever side by side.

The Path of Celestial Harmony

Beneath the vast celestial sphere,
We walk the path of sacred grace.
In unity, our hearts draw near,
Each step we take, a warm embrace.

The stars above, a guiding light,
They whisper secrets in the night.
In harmony, we seek the truth,
And find our strength in love and youth.

With every dawn, a chance to rise,
To breathe in hope, to shed our fears.
In nature's song, the soul complies,
A sacred dance through all the years.

Let kindness flow like rivers wide,
A gentle breeze that calms the storm.
In peaceful hearts, where love abides,
We find our way, our spirits warm.

So walk the path, both near and far,
With faith as light, let love ignite.
In celestial harmony, we are,
Forever bound by love's delight.

The Divine Thread of Existence

In silence woven, life's design,
A tapestry of fate and grace.
Each strand a story, yours and mine,
In the loom of time, we interlace.

The threads of joy, the threads of pain,
Weaving moments into one.
In every loss, in every gain,
The pattern stretches, never done.

Through trials faced and battles fought,
We find the strength to carry on.
With every lesson life has taught,
The thread grows strong, from dusk to dawn.

In love's embrace, we recognize,
Our stories blend, forever twined.
The divine thread before our eyes,
A sacred bond, eternally aligned.

So cherish every woven line,
In the fabric shared, we find our way.
With faith and love as the design,
The divine thread will always stay.

The Essence of a Guided Journey

In shadows deep, the spirit calls,
With whispers soft, through ancient halls,
The paths of faith, brightly shine,
As hearts entwine in love divine.

Each step we tread on sacred ground,
A purpose clear, in silence found,
The stars above, a guiding light,
Through darkest nights, toward the right.

In prayer we rise, as one we stand,
Together seeking heaven's hand,
With every breath, our souls renew,
In faith's embrace, we journey true.

The trials faced, our strength revealed,
In love's embrace, our wounds are healed,
For in this walk, we find our peace,
As guided spirits find release.

Rejoice in grace, let hearts be free,
In every moment, see the key,
For in this quest, the truth shall gleam,
The essence seen, in every dream.

The Pilgrim's Heart in Belief

The pilgrim's heart, with fervor beats,
Through winding roads, the journey greets,
In humble faith, we raise our song,
A chorus sweet, where we belong.

Each distant land, a story shared,
In every hand, the love declared,
With sacred fire, our spirits soar,
As every step is one of more.

In ancient scripts, we seek the way,
With each new dawn, a chance to pray,
Through trials faced, we learn to grow,
In belief's warmth, the light will show.

Through valleys low and mountains high,
The pilgrim's quest will never die,
For in the heart, a flame ignites,
In unity, we claim our rights.

The journey long, yet worth the while,
With humble grace, and faith's sweet smile,
In every soul, a story speaks,
The pilgrim's heart in love's mystique.

The Celestial Current of Life

In cosmic dance, the spirits flow,
A current strong, where rivers go,
With each heartbeat, a pulse divine,
In life's embrace, all souls align.

Stars above, like lanterns bright,
Guide weary hearts through endless night,
With every breath, we rise and fall,
In nature's song, we heed the call.

Through changing tides, our paths will weave,
In faith we trust, as we believe,
The harmony of life unfolds,
A sacred tale, eternally told.

In love embraced, we find our way,
Through every night, into the day,
The essence of a life in grace,
In the celestial flow, we find our place.

With open hearts, we brave the strife,
In every pulse, the truth of life,
For in this current, wisdom thrives,
The celestial path where spirit lives.

The Serenity of Chosen Paths

In quiet woods, where stillness reigns,
The chosen paths, like gentle chains,
With every step, let peace arise,
In whispered prayers, we touch the skies.

Through rugged trails, and fields so green,
In nature's heart, our souls are seen,
With every choice, we find our role,
The journey shared, the sacred whole.

Beneath the sun, or under stars,
The light of love, our guiding spars,
In harmony, we walk as one,
In life's embrace, our fears undone.

The path we tread, in wisdom's grace,
Each turn we take, a warm embrace,
For in the stillness, truth we find,
The serenity of hearts aligned.

In gratitude, we lift our song,
For every choice that leads us strong,
In unity, we rise and stand,
The serenity of this, our land.

Chasing Whispers of Eternity

In stillness, souls take flight,
Whispers echo through the night.
Hearts ablaze with gentle grace,
Seeking truth in sacred space.

The stars above might softly gleam,
Guiding us with a holy beam.
In shadows cast, we find the light,
Chasing whispers, holding tight.

Each prayer a thread, woven fine,
Connecting us to the divine.
Through trials fierce, we rise, reborn,
Chasing whispers like the dawn.

In quietude, we hear the calls,
Every tear, a sacred thrall.
In every heartbeat, grace bestowed,
Chasing whispers on the road.

With faith as wings, we soar above,
In search of peace, in search of love.
Eternity sings its blessed song,
Chasing whispers, where we belong.

The Radiance of a Gracious Path

In every dawn, a promise true,
The radiance shines, revealing you.
With gentle hands, we walk in grace,
Finding beauty in every place.

The winding way may bring us pain,
But love will guide us home again.
In shadows deep, His light will beam,
The radiance flows, a holy dream.

Steps of faith, though small they seem,
Lead us forth in the greatest theme.
Each blessing falls like silken rain,
The radiance bright, our sweet refrain.

With tender hearts, we seek to learn,
In every turn, our spirits burn.
The gracious path, though steep and long,
The radiance sings our sacred song.

Through trials faced with steadfast will,
The radiance guides, our hearts to fill.
Onward we march, hand in hand,
The gracious path, our promised land.

Following the Divine Call

In silence grows the sacred voice,
Inviting all to make the choice.
Every heartbeat, a gentle draw,
Following the divine call.

With open hearts, we pave the way,
To share the love, to heal the fray.
As stars unite in twilight's thrall,
Together we'll answer the call.

With every step, our spirits rise,
In faith we walk towards the skies.
Through valleys low and mountains tall,
We find our strength in the divine call.

A whisper stirs within our souls,
A promise kept, as time unfolds.
In unity, we shall not fall,
For we are one with the divine call.

With souls aflame, we journey forth,
In love's embrace, we find our worth.
Hand in hand, we hear time's thrall,
Following the path of the divine call.

The Promise Beyond the Veil

In every heart, a hidden flame,
The promise made, forever the same.
Through trials faced and darkness felt,
The promise dwells, our fears to melt.

Beyond the veil, where shadows flee,
Hope awaits, a mystery.
In every sigh, a breath of peace,
The promise reigns, our souls release.

In twilight's hush, we find our way,
The promise shines, a brighter day.
With open arms, we greet the light,
The promise beyond the veil, our sight.

Through paths unknown, the journey's made,
In love's embrace, we are remade.
For every tear, a joyous swell,
The promise whispers, all is well.

In sacred trust, we walk with grace,
Beyond the veil, we find our place.
The promise sung in a timeless tale,
Guides us home, beyond the veil.

Cartographer of the Celestial

In the heavens so vast and wide,
Stars align as destiny's guide.
Guiding souls through night's embrace,
Sketching paths in sacred space.

With each stroke, a journey unfolds,
Ancient tales in whispers told.
Celestial realms, a sacred weave,
In faith's fabric, we believe.

With compass set by grace divine,
We seek the light, our spirits shine.
Charting worlds unseen, unknown,
With every step, His love has grown.

Through trials faced and fears disarmed,
In prayer's embrace, we're safe, we're warmed.
A cartographer of the heart,
Mapping love in every part.

So let us wander, hand in hand,
Through life's journey, heaven's planned.
With faith as our eternal guide,
In sacred truth, we shall abide.

Pilgrimage Through the Soul's Landscape

Across the hills of silent prayer,
We tread with faith, a journey rare.
The landscape shifts from dark to light,
In every shadow, hope ignites.

With every step, our burdens shed,
In whispered truths, our spirits fed.
A pilgrimage of love's embrace,
The soul's yearning to find its place.

Through valleys deep, where sorrows weep,
We trust the journey, our spirits steep.
In hills of grace, we rise anew,
Each breath a promise, each heartbeat true.

In every moment, a sacred call,
To lift our hearts, to rise, to fall.
As pilgrims, we seek the divine,
In every flower, a love sign.

With arms open wide to the skies,
We welcome truth in every guise.
In unity, the path we trace,
A tapestry of endless grace.

Heaven's Map Revealed

In quiet corners of the night,
Heaven's secrets glow so bright.
Maps of stars and sacred signs,
In prayer we seek, in love we find.

Every whisper, a guiding flame,
Illuminates our hearts with name.
Each moment, a divine embrace,
In mystery, we find our place.

The compass spins, yet hearts align,
Navigating through the divine.
With faith as anchor, hope as sail,
We journey forth, we shall not fail.

In seeking truth, we walk the line,
Between the earthly and divine.
Heaven's map laid bare for us,
In love, we trust, in love, we must.

As paths converge, our spirits soar,
Each heartbeat sings, forevermore.
Heaven's map revealed with grace,
In unity, we find our place.

Wandering With a Purpose

In wandering hearts, a purpose lies,
With every step, the spirit flies.
Through valleys low and mountains high,
We seek the truth beneath the sky.

In moments lost, we find our way,
A purpose shines, come what may.
Each path we tread, a lesson learned,
In every challenge, hope, returned.

With every breath, the journey calls,
To rise again whenever we fall.
Purpose whispers, softly near,
In quiet moments, we can hear.

Through winding roads and endless seas,
We wander forth, with hearts at ease.
In faith's embrace, our spirits bloom,
Wandering souls dispel the gloom.

So let us walk with hearts aglow,
In love and grace, let purpose grow.
To wander with a sacred aim,
In life's great dance, forever claim.

Celestial Navigation of the Spirit

In the night, stars brightly gleam,
Guiding souls, like a dream.
With whispered winds, the heart will soar,
To realms of love, forevermore.

The heavens weep, the ancients sigh,
Beneath the vast, unending sky.
Each twinkle holds a truth divine,
As spirits search, their paths align.

Celestial maps, in silence drawn,
With every dawn, a new love's song.
The heart, a vessel, pure and wide,
Navigates the eternal tide.

In prayerful quests, we find our way,
In humble hearts, the light shall stay.
With faith we rise, like morning light,
A testament to love's pure might.

O seeker true, fear not the night,
For in the dark, the stars ignite.
With every step, the spirit knows,
The vibrant path where love bestows.

The Pilgrim's Map of Love

With every journey, love is drawn,
In every heart, a sacred dawn.
A map unfolds, in hands of grace,
Guiding pilgrims to life's embrace.

Upon the hills, where shadows play,
We walk the path, come what may.
With every step, love's fire ignites,
Illuminating darkest nights.

Through valleys low and mountains high,
The spirit whispers, never shy.
With open hearts, we search for truth,
In every moment, find our youth.

Together we tread, hand in hand,
In unity, we take our stand.
For love, a compass, leads us true,
In every breath, it starts anew.

The pilgrim's heart knows no defeat,
In love's embrace, we are complete.
With every tear, a lesson found,
In love's deep sea, our souls are bound.

Echoes of the Seraphic Guide

In sacred hush, the angels sing,
Soft echoes rise on heaven's wing.
With voices pure, they call us near,
To share the love that conquers fear.

They weave the threads of fate with care,
Reminding us that hope is there.
In gentle light, they cast their grace,
Upon our hearts, they leave a trace.

With every step, the echo flows,
As divine love eternally grows.
Through trials faced, they guide our way,
In wielding faith, we find our stay.

The seraphs watch, their eyes aglow,
In every shadow, their light will flow.
With open hearts, we hear their call,
In love's embrace, we find our all.

So let us dance in spirit's grace,
With seraphic guides in this sacred place.
Through love's sweet song, we journey wide,
And in each echo, we'll abide.

Trusting the Divine Wanderer

In the quiet of the morning light,
We find the path, our hearts take flight.
The Divine Wanderer leads the way,
Through fields of grace, we humbly sway.

With every step, uncertainty fades,
In trusting love, the spirit invades.
We walk by faith, not by sight,
Guided by love's eternal light.

In winding trails, the soul will yearn,
For whispers soft and lessons learned.
Through trials fierce, our spirits grow,
With each new dawn, more love to sow.

The Wanderer beckons, hearts aligned,
In every moment, grace entwined.
Through every storm and peaceful sea,
We find our strength, in unity.

With open arms and eyes that see,
The magic found in simplicity.
Forward we tread, with love our guide,
Trusting the path, with hearts wide.

The Light That Ever Guideth

In shadows deep, Thy light doth shine,
Guiding the lost, with love divine.
Through trials faced, we find our way,
Each step we take, in faith we stay.

With every dawn, Thy grace renews,
In whispered prayers, our hearts consume.
Thy beacon bright, in night so cold,
A promise kept, a truth we hold.

Though storms may rage, and fears may rise,
We lift our eyes to boundless skies.
Thy hand upon our trembling hearts,
In every pain, a new life starts.

The path ahead, unknown and vast,
Yet in Thy love, we find our past.
Forever held in sacred light,
We walk in faith, through darkest night.

In every moment, guidance flows,
The light of heaven, forever glows.
With thankful hearts, we sing in praise,
To Thee, O Lord, our voices raise.

The Unseen Hand of Providence

In every step, Thy hand we see,
The hidden ways of destiny.
Though trials come and shadows fall,
We trust, dear Lord, in Thy great call.

With gentle touch, our lives are led,
Through winding roads, by faith we're fed.
In moments still, our hearts align,
With every breath, Thy plan divine.

When hope seems lost, and dreams fade away,
In quiet strength, we find our way.
The unseen hand that guides our fate,
In love, we trust, and we await.

Through valleys low, and mountains high,
Thy grace uplifts, we learn to fly.
In every tear, a lesson found,
In every loss, Thy love surrounds.

The tapestry of life is spun,
With threads of peace, through trials won.
Our journey flows, a sacred dance,
In Providence, we find our chance.

Navigating the Waters of Grace

In waters vast, where waves may crash,
Thy grace, O Lord, our sails will dash.
Through storms we face, with hearts so bold,
In every trial, Thy story told.

With gentle waves, Thy love will steer,
In whispered winds, we feel Thee near.
Through tempest's roar, our spirits soar,
In tranquil hearts, we seek Thee more.

Each ripple holds a sacred truth,
An echo of our blessed youth.
In every tide, with faith we glide,
Thy mercy flows, our truest guide.

Across the shores of hope and grace,
We find, dear Lord, a warm embrace.
In every heart, Thy love shall reign,
Through waves of joy, and through our pain.

As stars align, and dreams take wing,
In harmony, our souls shall sing.
In waters deep, we find our way,
Navigating grace, come what may.

The Sanctuary Within

Amidst the noise, a quiet place,
A sanctuary filled with grace.
Within our hearts, where love abides,
In sacred space, the spirit guides.

Through trials faced, we seek retreat,
In whispered prayers, our souls complete.
The world outside may storm and sway,
But here in peace, our fears decay.

Each moment still, a treasure found,
In silence deep, our hearts unbound.
With every breath, a sacred vow,
In joyful trust, we live in now.

The sanctuary where hope arises,
A haven blessed with sweet surprises.
In light divine, we come alive,
Through every trial, we will thrive.

So when the world feels tempest-tossed,
Inward we turn, though all seems lost.
In sanctuary, our souls entwine,
With Thee, dear Lord, our love shall shine.

The Symphony of Spiritual Guidance

In silence speaks the gentle breeze,
Whispers of truth among the trees.
Each note a blessing from above,
Guiding the heart with purest love.

Through trials faced and shadows cast,
A melody flows, steadfast and vast.
In moments dark, the light breaks through,
Harmony found in the soul's view.

The stars align in sacred dance,
Inviting the seeker to take a chance.
With each heartbeat, wisdom flows,
A symphony only the spirit knows.

Let faith be the guide, steady and bright,
Illuminating paths in the night.
Together we rise, hand in hand,
In this grand orchestra, forever to stand.

So trust in the song, your spirit's grace,
A beautiful journey, at its own pace.
For in each note, a promise rings,
In the symphony of life, the soul sings.

The Sanctuary of Inner Knowing

In stillness, find your refuge deep,
Where truths are planted, and secrets keep.
A divine whisper, soft and clear,
Guiding the heart, casting out fear.

Within this space, the soul takes flight,
With every breath, embracing the light.
An altar built of hope and grace,
Here lies the timeless, sacred place.

The mind may wander, yet peace remains,
In the sanctuary, joy sustains.
Open the door, step inside,
Where love enfolds and spirits glide.

Beneath the surface, wisdom flows,
A river of light that eternally grows.
Trust in the peace that gently calls,
Within this haven, the spirit enthralls.

So linger here, and feel the glow,
Of the inner knowing that only you know.
Let silence speak, let stillness reign,
In the sanctuary, no more pain.

The Serene Voyage of the Spirit

Across the tides of time and space,
The spirit sails with gentle grace.
In every wave, the lessons learned,
A sacred journey, forever yearned.

With sails unfurled, the heart takes flight,
Navigating stars that shine so bright.
Each moment cherished, each glance divine,
In the voyage where spirits entwine.

The winds of change may test the course,
Yet trust the current, feel its force.
In every storm, a chance to grow,
The serene voyage, the soul's flow.

To distant shores, the heart will roam,
In search of truth, in search of home.
Embrace the journey, let go of fears,
For every step is worth the years.

And when the voyage finds its end,
The spirit knows it will transcend.
In unity found, all hearts align,
The serene voyage, a love divine.

Riddles of the Divine Voyager

In the depths of night, a question stirs,
What lies beyond the bounds of words?
In shadows cast, the truth remains,
A riddle wrapped in love's embrace.

The seeker wanders, heart in hand,
Searching for meaning in this land.
Every answer holds a hidden quest,
In the divine, the spirit rests.

With eyes wide open, the mystery unfolds,
In stories of old, the wisdom told.
Each puzzle piece in the grand design,
Crafting lessons that intertwine.

What is the essence of this endless roam?
The heart whispers softly, "You are home."
In every challenge, every choice,
The divine voyager finds their voice.

So ponder the riddles, seek and explore,
For in every question lies an open door.
Embrace the journey, the twists and turns,
In the dance of life, the spirit learns.

The Serene Path of Divine Clarity

In silence, whispers call my name,
Guiding me through shadows, free from blame.
The light above, a beacon bright,
Illuminates the way, dispels the night.

With every step, my heart aligns,
In peace I walk, where spirit shines.
The world may swirl with chaos near,
But in this path, I find no fear.

Each breath a prayer, each thought a hymn,
In harmony, my soul's not dim.
I trust the flow, a sacred stream,
In every moment, I find my dream.

Nature sings, a sacred song,
In the stillness, I do belong.
The universe unfolds its plan,
In divine clarity, I understand.

So onward I tread, with faith anew,
Embracing grace in all I do.
The path ahead is rich and vast,
In divine light, I stand steadfast.

A Journey Unseen by Mortal Eyes

A journey unfolds, beyond the sight,
Where shadows dance, and dreams take flight.
With each step taken, I learn to trust,
In the unseen realm, my soul adjusts.

Whispers of wisdom echo in the soul,
Guiding me gently to find my whole.
In prayerful quiet, I seek to find,
The beauty hidden, the truth entwined.

Through valleys deep and mountains high,
The spirit leads, as stars reply.
The path is woven with love's embrace,
In sacred spaces, I find solace.

Each moment a gift, a chance to learn,
In the journey unseen, my heart does yearn.
For every trial shapes my grace,
In this hidden realm, I find my place.

Eternal echoes softly guide,
In faith and hope, I will abide.
The journey unfolds, a dance divine,
In the unseen, my spirit shines.

The Sacred Dance of Direction

In rhythm and grace, the heart does sway,
The sacred dance leads night and day.
With every turn, the soul takes flight,
In the embrace of love's pure light.

Choreographed by divine design,
The steps align, the stars all shine.
With open arms, I join the song,
In the sacred dance, where I belong.

Each movement tells a story true,
Of grace and strength, old and new.
In the flow of life, I find my path,
In sacred rhythms, I escape wrath.

The drumbeat calls, the spirit thrives,
In every echo, my heart derives.
The sacred dance holds wisdom deep,
In every twirl, the soul will leap.

As shadows merge with the dawn's new light,
I find my place, my spirit bright.
In unity, the dance is whole,
A sacred rhythm for every soul.

In Search of Celestial Truth

With eyes turned upwards, I begin to seek,
The whispers of truth, the voice, though meek.
In every flower, in every tree,
A hint of heaven beckons me.

In stillness found within the night,
The stars above shine pure and bright.
Their gentle glow, a map from old,
Tales of love and grace unfold.

Through rivers wide, and mountains tall,
I wander on, answering the call.
Each step I take, in faith I trust,
In search of wisdom, pure and just.

The heart's yearning, a compass true,
In dance with shadows, I find the view.
The celestial truth, a light in hand,
Guides my spirit across the land.

So onward I walk, with hope in bloom,
In search of light, dispelling gloom.
The journey long, yet sweetly clear,
In the quest for truth, I persevere.

Beneath the Shadow of the Sacred

In the quiet night, we gather near,
Whispers of love, we hold so dear.
Under the stars, a guiding light,
Beneath the shadow, our hearts take flight.

Cloaked in grace, we find our way,
Finding strength in each word we say.
With hands clasped tight, we seek to know,
The sacred path where blessings flow.

Each promise made in reverent prayer,
Echoes through silence, lingers in air.
Bonded together, souls entwined,
In this stillness, our faith aligned.

Through trials faced and burdens borne,
In the depths of night, a new day's dawn.
A sacred embrace, we hold forth high,
In the shadowed light, we learn to fly.

So let us walk, with hearts aglow,
Beneath the sacred, where spirits grow.
In the gentle hum of life's sweet song,
We find our place, forever strong.

Cradle of Celestial Waters

In the cradle where waters gently sway,
Life is birthed anew, day by day.
Each droplet speaks of grace divine,
In celestial harmony, our hearts align.

Ripples dance on the surface wide,
Carrying whispers from deep inside.
A sacred stream where the lost can find,
The loving touch of the eternal mind.

Beneath the skies, in the depths below,
Faith flows freely, a radiant glow.
In the vibrant pulse of aquatic grace,
We gather strength in this hallowed space.

As rivers merge and paths entwine,
We seek the wisdom of the divine.
Every prayer cast upon the sea,
Echoes back in tranquility.

Together we float, in unity blessed,
In the cradle of waters, our fears are rest.
Through tides of sorrow, through waves of cheer,
We find our solace, knowing God is near.

The Divine Pulse of Existence

In the heartbeat of the cosmos bright,
Lies the song of creation, pure delight.
Each pulse vibrates with life's sweet thread,
In the divine dance, our spirits are fed.

From the mountains high to the oceans low,
Nature whispers secrets only few know.
In every heartbeat, in every sigh,
Echoes the truth of the Divine up high.

Life's rhythm flows in the stillness profound,
In the depths of silence, love is found.
As stars align and the heavens weep,
The pulse of existence stirs from sleep.

With open hearts, we traverse the flame,
In the sacred breath, we call His name.
Through every season, let life unfold,
In the divine pulse, we find our gold.

So let our voices rise in praise,
For the divine pulse that guides our ways.
In every moment, let love be our guide,
In the dance of existence, we bide.

Seeking the Blessings of the Way

On the path of light, we journey bright,
With humble hearts, we seek His sight.
Each step we take, each burden laid,
In the promise of grace, our fears will fade.

Through valleys deep and mountains tall,
In every challenge, we heed His call.
With faith as our compass, pure and true,
We walk this road, embraced anew.

In the sacred whispers of ancient trees,
We find the solace of the breeze.
Each leaf a blessing, every flower a sign,
In seeking the Way, our spirits intertwine.

For in the silence, the world will speak,
In moments of stillness, we grow meek.
Seeking the blessings bestowed from above,
In every heartbeat, we find His love.

So let us carry our truth with grace,
In the journey together, we find our place.
In the light of His guidance, we shall trod,
Forever seeking, hand in hand with God.

In Pursuit of the Infinite

In whispers soft, the heavens call,
A journey starts beyond the fall.
With faith as wings, we seek the sky,
Through sacred paths our spirits fly.

The stars above, they guide our quest,
In night's embrace, we find our rest.
Each prayer a step, each breath a tune,
We chase the light, we crave the boon.

Eternal truths, like rivers flow,
In gentle streams, our hearts do grow.
The infinite beckons, so we stride,
With hope ablaze, we walk beside.

In silence deep, the spirit wakes,
The heart rejoices, the soul it shakes.
For in this quest, the world takes shape,
And love, our guide, we shall escape.

To seek the vast, the boundless grace,
In every shadow, we find a trace.
For in the dance of time and space,
We find the Infinite's warm embrace.

The Harmony of Divine Guidance

In gentle winds, His whispers flow,
A guiding hand where'er we go.
With every step, in faith we tread,
For He's our light, where hope is spread.

The melody of hearts in prayer,
Resounds in stillness, lifts our care.
In unity, we find our song,
With grace and love, we all belong.

Through trials fierce, we stand in trust,
His faithful love, forever just.
In each dark night, the dawn will break,
And in His peace, our fears will shake.

In every loss, a lesson learned,
The path of faith is often turned.
Through storms we rise, with spirits bold,
In harmony, His truth unfolds.

Together bound, we walk this road,
With hearts aligned, we share the load.
For in this journey, hand in hand,
We find the strength, together stand.

The Lighted Way to Belonging

In every heartbeat, love's refrain,
A sacred bond that knows no pain.
With open arms, we find our place,
In light and warmth, we share His grace.

The tapestry of lives entwined,
In faith, we seek, in trust, we find.
Each story told, a thread of gold,
In unity, our hearts unfold.

On this bright path, we gather near,
Embracing joy, dispelling fear.
In every smile, in every tear,
The essence of belonging here.

As stars above in heavens gleam,
In loving kindness, we dream the dream.
For every soul is precious, bright,
In the lighted way, our hearts take flight.

Together, we rise, through dark and light,
In harmony, we'll win the fight.
For in this journey, hand in hand,
In love united, we take our stand.

The Ethereal Map of Love

Beyond the veil where shadows lie,
An ethereal map guides us nigh.
With every heartbeat, love's design,
In sacred lines, our paths entwine.

In whispered prayers, we share our dreams,
With open hearts, affection beams.
Through valleys deep and mountains high,
In love's embrace, our spirits fly.

Each winding road a story told,
In compassion's light, our hearts unfold.
With every touch, with every glance,
We find the strength in love's sweet dance.

Though trials come to test our will,
In love's embrace, we find the thrill.
For every heart is meant to glow,
On this vast map, love's river flows.

Together we walk, beneath the stars,
In every moment, healing scars.
For on this journey, take your part,
The ethereal map leads to the heart.

The Veil of the Infinite Journey

Through shadows deep, the path unfolds,
A tapestry of grace, in silence holds.
With every step, the spirit soars,
In search of truth, beyond distant shores.

The veil that hides the sacred sphere,
Whispers the secrets we long to hear.
In twilight's glow, the heart takes flight,
Awake, arise, to the dawn's soft light.

With faith as guide, the weary tread,
Each moment cherished, the soul is fed.
Through trials faced, and burdens borne,
A journey blessed, as new life's sworn.

In the night, where doubts may creep,
We find the strength, the courage to leap.
For every shadow holds a sign,
A beacon bright, that love defines.

And when the road feels dark and long,
Remember, child, you are not wrong.
For in the heart, the truth shall dwell,
A whispered love, a sacred well.

The Guiding Light of Conviction

In the depths of night, a flame does spark,
A beacon bright, dispelling dark.
With every doubt, a strength we find,
Conviction whispers, ever kind.

Through trials fierce, the heart may break,
But from the ashes, new hopes awake.
Each step we take, with faith we'll rise,
A path of glory beneath the skies.

The storms may howl, the winds may wail,
Yet in our souls, love shall prevail.
With every breath, a promise made,
In truth and light, we are remade.

Hold firm the light, let shadows fade,
In unity, our debts are paid.
For in conviction, we find our way,
A guiding star, both night and day.

And when the road ahead seems steep,
Fear not the darkness; it cannot keep.
For in the heart, truth ever glows,
A sacred bond, that forever grows.

Whispers of the Soul's Journey

In silence deep, the spirit sings,
A melody of hope, on hidden wings.
Through valleys low and mountains high,
The whispers call, do not deny.

Each echo leads the way to grace,
In every trial, we find our place.
The journey long, yet not in vain,
With every heartbeat, we break the chain.

Embrace the light, the warmth it brings,
For in our souls, the truth still sings.
Through every tear that we may weep,
A sacred promise, a vow to keep.

In the quiet hours, listen close,
For in the stillness, we might find most.
The whispers guide, the path is clear,
In the light of love, we conquer fear.

And as we walk this winding road,
Each step a treasure, a sacred code.
The soul's journey, forever blessed,
In the arms of grace, we find our rest.

The Light of the Faithful Traveler

Upon the road, the traveler treads,
With humble heart, and spirit spreads.
Each step a prayer, each pause a song,
In the dance of life, we all belong.

Through unfamiliar paths, we roam,
In search of solace, we find our home.
The light of truth, a constant guide,
In every wound, the love inside.

With open eyes, the world we see,
Reflecting hopes, and unity.
In every face, a story told,
Of faith, of love, of spirits bold.

And when the night begins to fall,
The faithful listen to the call.
For even darkness has its grace,
Within the light, we find our place.

Each traveler's heart holistically beats,
Together we rise, despite defeats.
In every journey, a sacred thread,
In the fabric of life, the spirit is fed.

Communion with the Celestial

In silence, we raise our hands,
Seeking light from distant lands.
Whispers of grace fill the air,
Hearts entwined in holy prayer.

Stars above, a guiding flame,
Each heartbeat echoes your name.
In this moment, time stands still,
Bound by love, we bend our will.

The universe sings with delight,
In your arms, the world feels right.
Breath of life, divine embrace,
In communion, we find our place.

With every tear, a lesson learned,
In the darkness, our souls burned.
Yet through fire, we rise anew,
Seeking visions pure and true.

In unity, we find our strength,
Together we journey the length.
With faith as our steadfast guide,
In your mercy, we abide.

The Pathway of Surrender

Upon the road, our burdens lay,
Each step leads us, come what may.
In trust, we place our heavy doubts,
Letting go of inner shouts.

With open hearts, we face the night,
Finding peace in the gentle light.
Every trial a sacred test,
In your love, we find our rest.

Let the winds of change blow free,
In surrender, we learn to see.
What was lost is now restored,
In your arms, we are adored.

As rivers flow, so shall we,
Moving onward, wild and free.
With every moment, grace unfolds,
In surrender, our hope holds.

Here in this sweet yielding grace,
We find ourselves in your embrace.
The journey taught us, love's a song,
In surrender, we all belong.

Signs Along the Pilgrimage

Amidst the hills, a whisper calls,
In nature's breath, the spirit thralls.
Every footprint, a story told,
In this quest, we are brave and bold.

The rustling leaves, the warming sun,
Guide our hearts till day is done.
In shadows cast, we see the way,
Each moment leads us to the day.

With every star that lights the night,
We find our path, our guiding light.
In the stillness, signs appear,
Gentle nudges leading near.

Wandering souls, we seek the truth,
In our hearts, there is eternal youth.
With every dawn, a chance to grow,
Every sunset, a chance to know.

Through valleys low and mountains high,
In love's embrace, we learn to fly.
These signs along our pilgrimage,
Fill our hearts with hope and sage.

The Sacred Tapestry of Purpose

In threads of gold, our lives entwine,
Woven by hands, divine design.
Each choice a stitch, each tear a seam,
In the fabric, we live the dream.

Through colors bright and shadows grey,
Our purpose shines, come what may.
In moments dark, we find the light,
In grace, our spirits take flight.

Every heart, a different hue,
In unity, we break through.
A tapestry rich, vast and wide,
In your love, we shall abide.

From frayed edges, we must mend,
In trust, the pieces we transcend.
Every challenge, a sacred thread,
In your wisdom, we are led.

In this sacred woven art,
Each strand reflects the human heart.
Together, we create the whole,
A masterpiece, the journey of the soul.

Milton Keynes UK
Ingram Content Group UK Ltd.
UKHW020039271124
451585UK00012B/933

9 789916 898819